T0161178

Still the Mind

Still the Mind

An Introduction to Meditation

Alan Watts

NEW WORLD LIBRARY
NOVATO, CALIFORNIA

New World Library
14 Pamaron Way
Novato, California 94949

Copyright © 2000 by Mark Watts

Editors: Mark Watts, Marc Allen
Cover design: Big Fish
Text design: Tona Pearce Myers

Library of Congress Cataloging-in-Publication Data
Watts, Alan, 1915–1973.
Still the mind : an introduction to meditation / Alan Watts.
      p.   cm.
1. Meditation. I. Title.
ISBN 1-57731-214-7 (alk. paper)
BL627.W38 2000
291.4'35—dc21

                                                       99-462340

First paperback printing, February 2002
ISBN-10: 1-57731-214-7
ISBN-13: 978-1-57731-214-7
Printed in Canada on acid-free, partially recycled paper
Distributed to the trade by Publishers Group West

20 19 18 17 16 15 14

*What I am really saying is that you
don't need to do anything,
because if you see yourself in the correct way,
you are all as much extraordinary phenomenon
of nature as trees, clouds, the patterns
in running water, the flickering of fire,
the arrangement of the stars,
and the form of a galaxy. You are all just like that,
and there is nothing wrong with you at all.*

— Alan Watts

CONTENTS

By Marc Allen

ALAN WATTS BECAME FAMOUS in the 1950s as a brilliant, intense intellectual, a former Episcopalian priest with a vast knowledge of both Eastern and Western religious and spiritual traditions. Unlike most of his peers, though, he embraced and actually practiced the various traditions he studied. His understanding, expressed through a great number of books and public talks, was peerless.

In the 1960s, he became a serious student of Zen Buddhism, and was a teacher — and eventually dean — at the American Academy of Asian Studies (now CIIS, the California Institute of Integral Studies). The popularity of his books and talks soared. He gave a weekly talk on San Francisco public radio that was broadcast nationally. A large number of people listened every Sunday morning; many considered it their church service.

Watts lived on a houseboat in Sausalito, just north of San Francisco, which became renowned as a center of endless discussions, parties, and meditation sessions, with famous and infamous spiritual leaders, gurus, intellectuals, writers, and others continually dropping by.

He continued to practice his meditation, and his writing and talks deepened. More and more, he was leading people into meditation and spiritual experience rather than just talking about it.

In the last years of his life, he left the houseboat and retreated to a small, isolated cabin deep in the woods. He spent nearly every morning alone, usually beginning with a Japanese tea ceremony followed by a period of meditation and contemplation. Then he would write.

His writing and speaking grew quieter and deeper. This book has been transcribed from recordings of several talks he gave in his later years. They show a maturity and an understanding of his subject that only comes after years of meditation. He had transformed over the years from a serious intellectual to a joyous, spontaneous lover of life.

His words are still leading-edge, as fresh today as when they were spoken many years ago. He is a writer and student and teacher who will be remembered, and this book shows us why:

He is able to use words to take us beyond them; he is able to instill in readers and listeners not only an understanding of meditation but an actual spiritual experience as well.

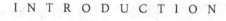

INTRODUCTION

BY MARK WATTS

I N THE BEGINNING of *Still the Mind,* Alan Watts mentions the gift he had been given — and it was a unique gift. Watts was able to take his readers and listeners on a journey beyond the often-ignored limitations of calculation and reckoning. Perhaps the greatest part of this gift was his ability to show us how to discover simple ways of getting out of the mental trap we create for ourselves.

In our modern society, it has become apparent that the power-based world — the world of politics, government, and international finance that influences all of us — has been absolutely hypnotized and driven crazy by words and by thoughts. We have become slaves to recurring patterns in an endless stream of words. Our political leaders talk incessantly about our many problems, but it's as if they're speaking a foreign language one might call "memorandese." Almost everyone has had the experience of watching a political debate and wondering afterward what on earth the candidates were talking about. To some degree, all civilized people are out of touch with reality because we fail to distinguish between the way things are and the way they are described. For politicians this dichotomy has reached extreme proportions, but it affects everyone. We confuse money, which is an abstraction, with real wealth; we confuse the idea of who we are with the actual experience of our organic existence.

During the sixties and early seventies, Alan Watts lectured at universities and blossoming growth centers across the country. To help his audiences better understand their connection with the world, he would describe in great detail the many ways that our organic existence inseparably connects us to the entire world. Starting when I was sixteen, and on into my early twenties, I followed along whenever I could with a portable tape deck, recording his talks.

Whether the title of his talk was *Ecological Awareness, The Psychology of Mystical Experience,* or *The Practice of Zen Meditation,* he would often return to the theme of the inseparability of man and world. It was something he grasped on a deep level and could invariably help his audiences understand. His essential point was that one's actual organic being is inseparable from the universe, but the distinct idea you have of this distinct wiggle of the whole universe, which you call your body, can very easily persuade you to accept the illusion that you are a separate entity.

One reason we fall for the idea of the separate, isolated self is that, even though we admire the beauty of the natural world, nearly everyone who has grown up in Western society has certain misgivings about actually living as an integral part of nature. Instead, we adopt certain conventions that allow us to live in modern society; we cultivate our consciousness in order to "rise above" the level of natural instinct.

At one extreme, we are rugged individualists who feel the need to conquer the physical world and claim new territory for mankind. But even those who do not try to dominate the world in a physical sense may try to overcome what they perceive as their animal nature through the repression of their natural desires. We see this manifested nearly everywhere in our culture in conscious attempts to adhere to abstract ideals of virtuous living.

But as Carl Jung wrote in his essay *The Stages of Life* that "instinct cares nothing for consciousness." Like my father, Jung believed that the problems we have are manifestations of our consciousness, and more particularly, the direct result of self-consciousness and our attempt to make things better. This is at the root of so many of the dilemmas we create in so many areas of our lives.

Look at the issue of ecology, for example: Although we sincerely want to get along with nature and not destroy it, we still see ourselves as people living separately from the natural world. We are still not a part of it, due to a trick of perception that many people have called the ego. In reality the whole problem is a mental trap, and the only way out of the trap is to wake up and simply *be* in the real world.

It is necessary therefore to experience the real world directly — but here we run into a problem because some people believe that the real world is the spiritual world and others believe it is the physical world. Both of these, however, are simply ideas, concepts. As Alan Watts and so many others keep pointing out, the real art of connecting with the universe is to *stop thinking,* at least from time to time.

Practicing the art of meditation or contemplation can help us stop the perpetual chatter that goes on inside our skulls. As my father often said, "A person who thinks all the time has nothing to think about except thoughts, and lives in a world of illusions." To the degree we can stop thinking and start experiencing, we are getting back to sanity, and to reality. In meditation or contemplation we can occasionally discover a state of consciousness that is truly not self-conscious. But the only way to do this is by allowing all attempts to mentally describe the world to cease. If we talk all the time, we won't hear what anyone else has to say, and if we think all the time, we will never experience the nature of our organic existence.

In the following pages we will explore what lies at the heart of what may still to this day be considered a new way of thinking and living. As Alan Watts and many others have understood, there is nothing new in it: We are connecting — or reconnecting — with an energy as old as the universe, and with a form of wisdom at least as old as the human race, well understood by indigenous peoples and brilliantly taught by Buddhists and Hindus.

In *Still the Mind,* we are taken on an experiential journey. By participating in the experiments suggested, you will find a way to get back in touch with the reality that exists beyond our thinking — the great, unified reality our thoughts are supposed to represent but can never capture or express.

Alan Watts says it much more clearly than I do — and it has been a gratifying experience for me to spend so much time with the hundreds of hours of his words that were recorded on tape. He is a speaker and writer whose voice has continued to have a great impact many years after his passing, and I believe it is well worth spending a few quiet hours from time to time with the book you're holding in your hands. You will see how he used words and thoughts to guide us beyond our words and thoughts, and you will come to understand that we are far greater, far more miraculous in our nature than our words can express.

PART I

THE ESSENTIAL PROCESS
OF THE WORLD

WHO WE ARE
IN THE UNIVERSE

I WAS TAUGHT when I was a little boy that it was good to be unselfish and loving, and I used to think that I should grow up to serve other people. But after a while I found out that unless one has something to give people, there is nothing one can do to help them. Just because I thought I ought to help, it didn't mean that I had anything to give.

Gradually, over the years, as I understood what it was that I had received of significance from the world, I realized that these things were never intended as gifts to be given in the usual sense of the word. However much one enjoys the song of birds, they are not singing for the advancement of music, and the clouds are not floating across the sky to be painted by artists.

In the words of a Zen poem,

> *The wild geese do not intend*
> *to cast their reflection*
> *The water has no mind*
> *to retain their image*

When a mountain stream flows out of a spring beside the road, and a thirsty traveler comes along and drinks deeply, the traveler is welcome. But the mountain stream is not waiting with the intention of refreshing thirsty travelers; it is just bubbling forth, and the travelers are always welcome to help themselves. So in exactly that sense I offer these ideas, and you are all welcome to help yourselves.

THREE WISHES

I am offering these words for your entertainment, and to entertain myself. I am not trying to improve you, and I really do not know how I would improve you. It would be imprudent for me to recommend any improvements, because one never knows how these things may turn out — and as they say, be very careful of what you wish for, because you may get it.

One of the problems when people ask for miracles is that they never know what the miracle they ask for ultimately involves. That is why magicians and genies always grant three wishes, so that after the first two you can always use the third one to get back to where you began.

What invariably happens is that with the first wish, things never quite work out as you expected. You may not realize what it may involve if you wish for a glass to be changed into gold, for instance. If we change the arrangement of the universe in such a way that glass becomes gold, you may suddenly find that your eyesight fails or you lose all your hair, because that might go with it. We do not understand all the interconnections between things, because in reality what we call "things" are not really separate from each other. The words and the ideas about them separate them from each other, but they are not separate. They all go with each other, inter-connected in one vast vibratory pattern, and if you change it at one point it will be changed at all sorts of other points, because every vibration penetrates through the entire pattern.

WHY DO YOU BELIEVE?

You never really know what is going to happen, and therefore I would not presume to say that you ought to be different than the way you are. I am not a guru, in the sense of a spiritual teacher or an authority from which you may expect something more than what you have. When you confer spiritual authority on another person, you must realize that you are allowing them to pick your pocket and sell you your own watch.

How can you be certain with any great teacher (or scripture for that matter) that they know what they say they know? You may believe in a religion; that is a choice you have made. But how do you know, and why do you believe?

If you believe in something simply because the Bible says it is true, for instance, you do so because you believe that the Bible has the authority to tell you it is true. You may well say that your fathers and mothers and all sorts of reliable people believed it, and therefore you have accepted it on their authority. If you are curious, however, you will also ask, "How did they know it was true?" Did they, by their light and example, show that they were enormously improved because of their belief?

If we look at human history with a clear eye, we see that over an appallingly long period of time people have not improved very much despite their religions and ideals. When you become a grandfather with five grandchildren as I am, you realize that you are just as stupid as your own grandfather was because you still look at things from your own limited position. And although my grandchildren may think that I am a wise and venerable man with a beard, I know that I am still a child, and I feel pretty much as I have always felt. So when you set someone up as an authority, never forget that the belief that you have in this authority is just your opinion.

IT RESTS ON OUR AUTHORITY

When De Tocqueville said that the people get the government they deserve, he was quite right. We allow the government, whether it be political or spiritual, to get away with it, and so it rests on our authority. This is true also of God. If you believe in God — that God is good, or that God is God at all — it is your opinion. And so God derives from you, and therefore this thought has some very peculiar implications with regard to the government of the universe.

Awareness of the source of spiritual authority — understanding that it comes from us, from the people — may imply that there is some sort of democracy in the kingdom of Heaven. Of course it does not overthrow God, except in the sense of a certain kind of God, and most people do not realize that there can be many quite different ideas of God.

God does not have to be a monarch; there can also be an organic god. There are also personal and impersonal gods, and there are gods that are neither personal nor impersonal. There are gods that exist and gods that do not exist, and there are gods that neither exist nor do not exist. But whatever you believe God is, it always goes back to *you.*

What Does Consciousness Rest Upon?

When his disciples approached the great Hindu sage Sri Ramana Maharshi and asked, "Guruji, who was I in my last incarnation?" he would answer, "Who wants to know?"

When they asked, "Guruji, how does one attain liberation?" he would reply, "Who is it that wants to attain?"

Who is asking the question? It always gets back to you, where it all begins — and what is that? Of course we might think we know who we are — we have been told who we are, and we bought the story we were told.

So you can't really blame anybody else for what you think of yourself. You can't go way back, in a sort of psychoanalytical way, and find the causation for what you are now. The answer is not in the behavior of your parents, or in your peer group, or whatever your situation was when you were a child, because the universe doesn't work that way. Instead it works the other way: It goes backward into the past from you, because you started it. And so when you blame somebody else for putting you into your current situation, it merely means that you have defined yourself incorrectly. Perhaps you have defined yourself as being limited to your conscious attention, and limited to your voluntary musculature. But is that all there is? Is that the real you?

What does consciousness rest upon? Have you ever asked yourself that question?

WHO ARE YOU?

Consciousness does not illumine the lamp from which it shines, just as a flashlight doesn't shine on the battery that powers it. When you make a decision, does that come from somewhere other than you? No, it comes from the depths of you, of which you are not really aware. You encompass far more than anything you know about in a conscious way.

But we are so used to thinking of "I" as simply the center of our consciousness, and the center of our will, that we ignore (or are *ignor*ant of) most of ourselves. When you think of a particular person, what do you think of? Suppose I say, "Think of your uncle," or "Think of your mother." What instantly comes to mind is their face, because we are most accustomed to seeing photographs and images of faces. When we see images of the president, most often it is the president's face, the head and shoulders, and only occasionally is the whole body seen.

What do you think of when you think of a flower? In the same way, you think mostly of the blossom, sometimes of the stalk, and occasionally of the whole plant. But very rarely when we think of a flower do we think of the flower out in a field. We would say, "That's more than the flower. The flower is not the field." But is that so? Where would the flower be without the field?

I can say in words, "The flower grows in the field."

In words I can chop the field off and say, "The flower grows," and the phrase will still make sense. However, it will not make sense in nature. If I take the field away from the flower, the flower cannot grow. The flower is connected with the field in a very deep way, and so in the same way a person is not just their head. The head has to go with the body, and the body has to go with a social and natural environment — but we never think of in that way. We know it is all there, but it doesn't come to mind automatically.

So who are you? And who decides on the limits of an organism? Who are you that gives spiritual authority to somebody else, and then pretends, "Of course it does not come from me. I bow down because I know that person really knows."?

Now the Buddhists have a very funny trick when it comes to bowing, because Buddhists do not have the idea of a supernatural authority that watches over them. So why, then, do they bow when they pay respect to a Buddha? Why do they bow when they meet you, and greet you so reverently? Bowing is paradoxically the act of a king, because it confers authority. The one who bows sets the revered image on its pedestal, and if there were no one to bow, there would be no image on the pedestal.

You put it there, but again you would ask, "How could it be so that what puts the authority up there is just poor little me, who is neurotic, or sinful, and doesn't really even understand what's going on?" But fundamentally the you that does this is the greater you, which is not just the activity of consciousness but the whole activity that expresses itself as you sit here and read this page. And what is it that expresses itself as you read? And what am I that is called Alan Watts and is offering these ideas?

I stated in the beginning that I am doing all this for entertainment, and I meant it. But who is it that is doing this for entertainment? If I say, "Alan Watts is a big act," who is it that puts on this act?

To try to trace the answer down, we might go to an astrologer and ask, "Who puts on the act?" "Well," he would say, "Where were you born, and at what time?" And he would go and look up the positions of the stars and the planets, and then he would draw a picture of my character, which just happens to be a very crude picture of the universe.

"There you are," he would say. "But I see you've drawn a picture of the universe," I would reply. That may be a surprise to him, because he probably thinks of the influences of the stars and of the planets as something that affects me, and that implies a certain separation between the bodies that cast the influences and the puppet that is influenced. But does the root of a flower influence the flower as something fundamentally different from it? No, surely the root and the flower are one process, and like your head and your feet it all goes together. In that sense then, the universe, and what you or I do, all goes together, and so that picture of the universe is really a picture of you.

We may not recognize ourselves because we think of ourselves as a chopped-off piece surrounded by our skin, and therefore we see ourselves in a rather impoverished way. And this form of perception is almost automatic. We think of ourselves as separate beings who stand alone and move through all sorts of different places but are cut off from the environment.

As a result we have an underlying feeling of alienation, of not really belonging in this universe, and we feel that we are being confronted by something that does not give a damn about us. It was here long before us, and will be here long after we are gone. We come into this world for a brief span as a little flash of consciousness between two eternal darknesses. Of course during our lives all sorts of other things go on, but nevertheless the feeling that haunts almost everybody is that this "I" is an orphan, here on a visit, and we don't feel that we really belong here.

In the same way, what do you feel when you look out at those galaxies? If you go out into a desert or up in the mountains where the sky is clear, you see this colossal affair that you are involved in. It makes a lot of people feel very small, but it shouldn't. It should make you feel as big as it is, because it is all inseparably connected with what you call *you*.

This tremendous whirling of energy is exactly one and the same energy that is looking out of your eyes, that is running along inside your brain, that is breathing, and that makes noises when you talk. The whole energy of the universe is coming at you and through you, and you are that energy.

THE NATURE OF ENERGY

"Well," we say, "but surely we die, and we disappear, we turn into dust, and this will go on long after I am gone." The whole nature of energy, however, is that it is a vibration, and a vibration is a wave, and a wave has a crest and a trough. It is like a pulse, it goes on and it goes off, and everything goes on and off.

Things like light go on and off so quickly that you can't see the off, because by definition on is always a little bit more noticeable than off. It is positive, whereas off is negative.

The outside of things is vibration, but because it goes very fast we don't quite sense it, and therefore it seems constant or solid, like the blades of an electric fan. This is true of light and also true of sound, but when you hear a very deep sound it vibrates noticeably. You can hear the texture in it; you can hear the vibrations

31

going on and off. When you hear a great pipe organ, the whole building shudders with these vibrations. We barely notice most of the pulses, however, including the slower pulses created by the turning of the earth, the cycles of the tides, or the coming and going of the equinoxes. These are very slow vibrations, but they always go on, and then off.

We are aware of these changes only because of the contrast within them. Of course you would not know something was on if it did not occasionally go off, and you would not know it was off if it did not sometimes go on. So I have often asked the question "How would you know you are alive unless you had once been dead?"

WHERE WOULD YOU BE WITHOUT NOTHING?

Where were you before you were born?

Where will you be when you die?

We may think we will become nothing, but what we don't realize is that nothing, in its own way, is as important as something. Where would you be without nothing? What is the background to being if it is not nonbeing?

You have to have nothing to have something. It is so simple, but nobody sees it because it is fundamental to Western philosophy that out of nothing comes nothing. But how can that be? According to our logic, in order for something, or someone, to come out of nothing, there must be some kind of hidden structure inside nothing. It must contain some sort of inner workings out of which something comes. But this is not the case at all. The whole point is that there is no concealed structure, and it is just because it is honest-to-goodness plain nothing that something comes out of it. That is elementary logic, but no one sees it because everybody is afraid of nothing.

People think, "Well, if it's nothing, it will never be something again, because that's going to be the end." The theologians get this mixed up too, and even someone like Saint Thomas Aquinas believed that out of nothing comes nothing, and then he said, "God created the world out of nothing." He made a mistake because he tried to identify God exclusively with being — and of course you cannot have being without nonbeing.

The Hindus understand this, as well as the Buddhists, who inherited their philosophy and mythology. They say God is neither being nor nonbeing; it is what they have in common. Yet nobody can say what that is, and still you know perfectly well that being and nonbeing go together, like an inside and an outside, a front and a back, a top and a bottom. Being and nonbeing are polarities, like the North and South Poles. What is in between?

Nobody really knows, because you can only know what you can compare with something else. You can know something only because you can compare it with nothing, and vice versa, but nobody knows what to compare with that which is common to both something and nothing.

It is for that same sort of reason that you cannot see for yourself the color of consciousness. What's the color of eyesight? We know all of the colors because they are different from each other. We see different colors in a mirror, but what is the color of the mirror?

We may say, "Silver" — but it isn't really. Although a mirror will reflect a silver spoon as something different from something else, the mirror is a noncolor. We can't compare it with any other color, and so it is transparent to our consciousness. And like your consciousness, and like space, it is a big nothing.

Most people treat space and consciousness as if they were not there, yet suppose there wasn't any space, only solid. There would be no outside the solid, and no one would know if it was round or square because there would be nothing to compare it to, and it would be all there would be.

It would appear rather dense, but of course most of what we call something is largely nothing when you get down to atoms. Whatever it is they are really made of is vast distances apart, and when we get to the inner structure of atoms, we find precious little there. It is a lot of nothing — and this nothing turns out to be very powerful stuff.

EVERYTHING GOES AROUND

In order to have room to move around, you have to have a void to move around in, and moving around is energy, which is definitely something. So that is the sort of thing we are in, and that is the sort of thing we are. We are not just *in* it, we *are* it, and it vibrates, it oscillates, and it goes around.

The cycles are not just simply wave motions or undulations, they are also cycles of a circular kind. Everything goes around, just as when we dance we go around — and it is tremendously important to get hold of this principle of going around. We are in a phase of the life of mankind when we seem to have forgotten that cyclic quality; instead of going around we all think we are going somewhere, and that implies there is somewhere else to go. But as I wander along, I can't help but wonder where that other place would be.

HIGHER ORDERS OF BEING

In the same way, when we think of evolution, we think of a scale and of a hierarchy of different sorts of beings. We might think, for example, that above us there are angels, and then gods, and then Buddhas with attending bodhisattvas going up to we know not what heights of amazing human development. And then we think that below us are the other mammals, perhaps demons, insects, bacteria, plants, rocks, down, down to we know not what depths.

So we congratulate ourselves and say, "How great it is to be human and not to be a cat, not to be a rose, and not to be a fish." And we think how much better it will be when we can get to be angels. We human beings are very conceited, and we think we can get up there and be gods or Buddhas.

But how do you know that you are a higher order of being than a potato? What do you really know about potatoes anyway? You probably have never studied potatoes beyond knowing how to cook and eat them. That's probably about it. But have you ever thought about how a potato feels?

"Well," you say, "it doesn't feel, it's only a potato, it has nothing to feel with." But wait a minute. When you put a lie detector on a potato — some kind of skin response machine — it certainly registers, and its readings change when you do certain things. If you prick the potato, or shout at it, it will flinch. As a matter of fact, if you learn how to turn on your alpha waves and you sit beside a plant, you will find that it will pick up those alpha waves. So maybe plants are not so stupid after all.

"Well," we might say, "how can it be? It has no civilization. It has no house. It has no automobiles. It has no pianos, no art galleries, and no religion."

But the potato might say, "I don't need them. It's

you poor uncivilized human beings who have to have all this crap around you to tell you who you are and what it's all about. You are messy and inefficient, and you are cluttering up the planet with your culture. But I, the potato, have it all built into me."

"Well," we might say, "that's impossible, because you are stuck in one place all the time. How can you know anything about the world?"

But the potato doesn't need to go running around because its sensitivity extends all over the place. And so it might say, "I want to introduce you to a few things. There is my neighbor over here, the thistle. Have you ever seen how my thistle neighbor gets around? It has tiny seeds with down sticking out all over them, and when the wind comes these seeds float off into the air. And my neighbor the maple tree has little helicopters it sends off, and they spin in the air and fly away. And then I have a friend the apple tree, and it has fruit that is so delicious that the birds like it. They eat the apple and swallow the seeds, then they fly away and when they drop the seed it is sown."

These are incredible devices. Others have burrs that stick in the hides of deer, and they carry these seeds around. "This is one of the ways we get around and we spread our people so that we aren't all crowded together and don't strangle ourselves."

The potato would go on to explain, "But this is only

the beginning of the extraordinary things that we do. We have vibrations going on inside our fibers that are quite as good as anything invented by your Bach and Mozart. We enjoy this, and although you may think we are not doing anything because we just sit here all the time, we are vibrating, and we are in ecstasy. We are humming to the great hum that is going on everywhere."

Your plants may be in such an advanced state of consciousness that, unknown to you, angels are growing in a flowerpot at your door. Unbeknownst to you they may have a great deal to do with the way you think.

Consider also that the humble fly may be extremely intelligent too. With all those eyes he sees a complex relationship of perspectives, and with the ability to walk upside down on the ceiling he may have a certain perspective that is far beyond ours. Whatever do flies do when they buzz? What is it all about? We don't know, because we don't even how know to begin to study them.

It took many years to find out that bees communicate with each other by dancing, and that was such a shock that one entomologist at UCLA said, "I have the most passionate reluctance to accept this evidence."

It is a shock to find out that dolphins, for example, may be more intelligent than people, and that so-called killer whales are a very intelligent kind of dolphin. Look at those creatures. They are mammals, and it is said — although we are not sure if this is true — that they once lived on the land. Apparently they decided that being on the land is a pretty stupid way for a mammal to live, and they said, "Let's go skin diving."

They said, "You really don't have to do much for a living, and you can dance and play." And so dolphins spend most of their time simply fooling around — and they fool around in very complicated ways. If we were dolphins, we would call this art.

When we practice any art, we are in a way just fooling around. We mix a lot of paint and make beautiful patterns on flat surfaces or on textured surfaces. We put together all kinds of boxes with pluckable wires, little tubes that we can blow our breath through, and enormous tubes that we blow breath through mechanically. We stretch great taut skins that we bang with our fists or with sticks, and do all kinds of other things.

When a symphony orchestra gets up on a stage, it is essentially just a lot of baboons blowing through holes, and yet this is something very important. There is a hush, the concertmaster comes in, and everybody applauds and sits down. The concertmaster then summons the orchestra into being, and people in their tiaras and pearls and ties sit back because this is culture and this is very serious. The whole atmosphere of the concert hall is very proper, like a church.

It is a little different when a rock band takes over, and there is a light show and everything is just blowing.

This is authentic music, and it is very important music. Perhaps this is the continuation of the great Western tradition. The concert hall is good for classical music, but as the new artists take over with their rather sophisticated new music, musicians like the Beatles and the Grateful Dead continue the tradition, but it is done in a different spirit. That music is a celebration, and there is nothing sedate about it. It's music to groove with, to be right there with, because you are not pretending that you are doing something important in a solemn sense. You are doing something important because you are right in the belly of things, and you're moving with it.

All of the vegetables understand this, and so from their point of view they are very highly evolved beings. Perhaps they don't consider us inferior beings, and just regard us as something different, but we are very unfair to vegetables. When at last a human being approaches the end of life and lapses into a coma, we say, "Poor old so-and-so, he's just a vegetable." Or when somebody is lazy, we say, "They're just vegetating."

Now that shows a lack of compassion toward vegetables. The word "compassion" means to feel with, or to have passion with. If you have compassion for vegetables, or for flies, or mushrooms, or viruses, what it means is that you have put yourself in their position. When you begin to really empathize, you discover that they think of themselves as people, and they have just as much right to think that they are civilized and cultured as you and I do.

So what does that do to our perception of an ordered universe? Think about it for a moment in human terms. For one thing, most of the people we call primitive are far less violent and less diabolical than we are as a society. They live more peaceable lives, and even though the tools they use are not as developed or complex as ours, these are very dignified, civilized people. They certainly are not savage.

Many primitive peoples look at us with grave concern. They don't regard us as civilized at all. Instead they view us as a rather serious menace to the planet, because we are out of touch with the ecology of nature, and tend on the whole to be extraordinarily miserable. Some of the richest places I know of are full of wealthy people who are really amazingly miserable because, despite their tremendous resources, they are always worrying about their health, their taxes, politics, or losing their money. You can always worry about something if you are the worrying type, and it doesn't matter how rich you are or how poor you are.

A Place Called You

As you carefully observe the cycles of life, a very strange kind of relativity begins to take root in your consciousness. Everywhere on a sphere is the same place, because there is as much east of you as there is west of you, and by the same logic, any point on the surface of the sphere is the center of the circle. Furthermore, if we live in a curved space-time continuum, any planet can be regarded as the center of the whole universe, and therefore any person on a planet stands in the situation of God — as that circle whose center is everywhere and whose circumference is nowhere. So when you want to become something more than you are, different from what you are, or higher than where you think you are, all that means is that you haven't discovered where you are, and you are under the illusion that there is somewhere else that you ought to be besides here.

What we are engaging in here is a journey to the place where we are, and I would like to describe to you some of the peculiarities of this journey. It is a sort of *Alice in Wonderland* story, because it is full of paradoxes.

If I say, "We are going on a journey to where we are, a journey to the center of the universe and to the middle of space and time, and it's a place called you," people will invariably begin to pass judgment about one's progress along the way. They will say things like, "I think this person is more aware than somebody else. He's more there than so-and-so is."

Then we begin to think about the stages one goes through in getting to be more where they are than they were before. You find this particularly in sophisticated circles, where people are concerned with spiritual and psychological development, and with religion. Some very curious games are played, and many of them are forms of spiritual one-upmanship. People become concerned with being more humble than other people.

PASSING JUDGMENTS

Suppose we see somebody who has a reputation, either deserved or undeserved, for being "spiritually evolved." That is the sort of phrase that is usually used. But if they get influenza and feel very sick, people shake their heads and say, "If so-and-so were really spiritual, they wouldn't be affected by sickness."

We have a funny notion in our heads that truly spiritual people are made of cast iron, that they are not sensitive, so that if you bang them about it won't affect them. But as the great Sixth Patriarch of China pointed out, you must learn to distinguish between a living Buddha and a stone Buddha, because if a buddha was simply one who was not affected by anything, then lumps of wood and pieces of stone would be Buddhas. And perhaps they are in their own way, but that wasn't the point he was making. His point was that if you think that the greatest ideal in life is to be invulnerable, then you are on your way to becoming geological rather than spiritual.

This kind of spiritual geology is very prevalent if you

know spiritual people as well as I do. I perpetually hear tales of people insisting that "my guru's better than yours." This goes on insufferably, whether it is my minister, my church, my society, or my own organization. I have heard all the reasons why, and I have heard people putting down other teachers and gurus, saying how dreadful it is that such and such a Zen master made them do so-and-so. Or we hear of the yogi who is a drunk, or sleeps with his students, or gambles, or drives cars too fast.

A great many spiritual people in this country are actually crypto-Protestants and still believe strongly in the Protestant ethic. Therefore they pass all of these judgments, despite the fact that the founder of the Christian religion said, "Judge not that you be not judged."

ALL THE DIFFERENT PERFORMANCES OF THE UNIVERSE

If you look at all the religions and all the different kinds of practices that people are doing in the same way that you look at different kinds of vegetables and different kinds of flowers and insects and butterflies, you will see that while yogis are assuming one perspective and Baptists are assuming another, what they are all really doing is a different kind of dance — and you can accept this, and look at it with absolute amazement, and say,

"Wow, look at all these different performances this universe is doing."

If you do this, you tend to stop griping and arguing about which one is the right one. Of course, you may not accept all of the performances entirely, you may not agree with their points of view. I must admit that I have some prejudices. I don't like the flavor of some Bible Belt religions, because I find them exceedingly depressing. I also don't like boiled onions; they're distasteful as well.

On the other hand, I can worship with the Roman Catholics, and the Episcopalians, and Theosophists, and Hindus, and Muslims, and feel perfectly at ease because I find that they are all doing the same thing in different and fascinating ways. Sometimes I draw the line, but I know when I do that it is nothing more than a personal prejudice, and I am entitled to some because I am human.

After all, to be human you have to have within you a touch of rascality. When God created Adam, he put in him just a touch of the wayward spirit, in the same way that one adds a little salt to a stew. If this slight oddity, this bit of unpredictability, had not been there, nothing would ever have happened, because Adam would never have tasted the apple.

A Pinch of Rascality

Once, Carl Jung felt that he had met a man with no human failings at all, and he was terribly disturbed, because it made him feel guilty. He thought that he should probably take a closer look at himself. Then a day or two later Jung met the man's wife, and he ceased to worry about it. It wasn't because she had said, "You should know my husband is very difficult to live with." That wasn't the story at all. Instead, the wife embodied all the things that were repressed in her husband, because when you live together that intimately you begin to share your psychic life. So if one becomes too much of a light, their partner may grow compensatory and become a shadow, and vice versa. So there has to be the element of rascality — but not too much, just a pinch of it.

When I come across somebody who does not appear to have it, especially so-called spiritual people who are very pure and sincere, I always suspect they are unconscious of human nature. There is something about these solemn purists that makes me feel uncomfortable, because I like people I can let my hair down with.

THE HIERARCHY OF LIFE

You may find this is disconcerting, however, because then you begin to wonder, "Is there no perfect human being? Isn't there somebody up there, a great being who we can all look up to and respect, or are saints and saviors pretty much like anyone else?"

When you look closely at the idea of the hierarchy

of life, you realize that even someone as remarkable as Jesus Christ — who from a Buddhist point of view would be considered a great bodhisattva — can emerge at any level. According to the Buddhist idea of reincarnation, we have all occupied every position in the hierarchy, or on the Wheel of Becoming, as the Buddhists call it, since the image of time they use is a wheel. In this view, by moving around the wheel, you eventually realize that every position to which you can shift is the same position you were always in. While you are shifting you may feel there is a change going on, but once you have settled into your new position, it feels like any other settled position always felt. From the inside we know what it feels like to have a settled position because from time to time we can change — but, as the French say, the more it changes, the more it remains the same.

We who live in a fidgety culture are apt to feel that this is an awfully boring philosophy, and that we are not going to get anywhere because there is no real progress. But, on the other hand, suppose there is a possibility of real advancement and improvement. Use your imagination to the best of your ability, and figure out exactly, and in detail, where you would rather be, and who you would rather be than who you are.

If you work on this for a while, somebody who is ingenious enough will always be able to point out to you that you have left something out, and that there is something else you could improve upon. You can go on and on, and as you go about this imaginative creation of the perfect life you will eventually realize that what you are really doing is extending power.

The process is very much like the people who are now working on gene manipulation so that man can direct the future of evolution and we can breed intellectual Einsteins, physical Elizabeth Taylors, and moral Sister Teresas. All of these people had extraordinary direction as human beings by virtue of their integrity and ingenuity, and so some people may look at this idea and think it would be just great. But look how we have extended our power now. We may think it would be good to be in charge of evolution, but along comes the old problem of the three wishes again. How do we know which way is really better?

When human beings attempt to take charge of evolution, they do so using their minds and a kind of consciousness that scans the world and looks at everything serially — but the problem is that the world itself is not serial. The world is what we call multidimensional, which is to say that everything is happening all together everywhere at once, and going along much too fast for us to take adequate cognizance merely through a scanning procedure. Because scanning is confined to linear limits, it always leaves things out, and these things may be very important.

That is why, as I pointed out before, turning the glass into gold may mean that your eyesight will fail or your hair will fall out. When we bring about change with our quite limited vision, and when we change people by altering their genes, we certainly will have a new situation, but it will not necessarily be any better, because we are unable to see in advance the fullness of the role that every individual will play.

In terms of projecting power, you will see that the geneticists' power is limited because they have a limited view. If we decide to give them all the computers they need to add it all up so that they will have a complete view of life, we are then placing ourselves in a position to control life on the planet. This is to be the final creation, and we are trying to carefully arrange it with our seemingly vast intellect and omnipotent consciousness. We are to be the master magicians; we are to have complete control over ourselves, and nothing is to happen that is not in accordance with our will.

Yet suppose we do all this, and suppose we have even managed to will our will so that it is always a good will. I am not quite sure how we would know it was a good will unless there was a possibility for bad will, but suppose we have managed. Ultimately, you must ask, "Do I want to be in that kind of situation?" In other words, think of where those directions we speak of as progressive are really going, and extrapolate on them.

Perhaps you will say, "Of course I wouldn't do that, because I realize I'm never going to get there." But even so, why are you even heading in that direction? Are you sure it's a better direction to go in? After all, we kill more people with cars than we do with wars, and you have to think about things like that. I am not arguing that we should not have technological developments, but perhaps it is shortsighted to conclude automatically that they are improvements. They may not be improvements at all in the long run — and so it is very important to consider whether you want to control the direction in which you are heading.

Full of Surprises

Inwardly, do you really and truly want to have power over everything that occurs within the sphere of your consciousness? Perhaps, speaking as a man, I would like to cast a spell over a woman so that she would become exactly as beautiful as I could conceive beauty to be, and so that every inflection of her voice and gesture would obey me like a violin under the hand of a perfect master. I would entirely direct her actions, and although in her every action she would be my dream, I would quickly begin to worry about this Frankenstein woman. I would think that perhaps there was nobody home, and that all I had done was to create a machine. When I think about it, what I really want is for her to do something that I don't expect.

That is one of the reasons why it is so nice when we have an occasion to give gifts. We love surprises, because a surprise means there was someone else there, someone who made it fun by doing something that we could not have predicted.

I've heard people who think that in the future, due to our psychic development, we are all going to be able to read each other's minds. Through direct transference from one mind to another we will have access to everybody's thoughts, and there will be no privacy left. Of course, since everybody will be completely transparent to everyone else, we won't be able to surprise each other. Personally I am not looking forward to that kind of world, because I am afraid it will be quite devoid of spontaneity. We may lose that little element we call vitality.

Now this may sound as if I am saying the best sort of thing is not a universe where we realize that there is a profound underlying unity through all things, but rather a universe that is pluralistic, that is not one at all. Certainly it may be said that one of the best parts of life is having lots of separate things all surprising each other, but I see still a different scheme.

The world I see is what we might call *unity in diversity*. What we call *self* and what we call *other* are like something and nothing. They are fundamental polarities, which — just because they contrast with each other — have something in common. We cannot say what it is, though, and therefore our world will always be full of surprises.

CHAPTER TWO

MEET YOUR
REAL SELF

WE HAVE STARTED out on a journey together to the place where we are. It's good to reflect, at some point along the way, on the futility of a certain kind of power game we play with our energy.

THE FUTILITY OF POWER GAMES

There are two kinds of games — the game you play to win and the game you play to play. There is a difference between the two, in the same sense as there is a difference between traveling to get somewhere and traveling just to travel, which we might call wandering.

There is a difference between motion with the objective of changing place and motion with the

53

objective of dancing. All those forms of energy that are moving to dance, or traveling to wander, are joyous manifestations of energy. On the other hand, all those forms of energy that have us moving to get somewhere tend to become frantic, and have a quality of urgency that moves us faster and faster until we simply can't go fast enough to accomplish the object. Even when it comes to practicing meditation, people keep asking about the fastest way, and they want to know how long it is going to take.

Nishkarma means action or doing (karma) without attachment, especially without attachment to the results of action. Nishkarma is the whole point and message of the Bhagavad Gita, or "Song of the Lord," which consists of the instructions of the charioteer Krishna to the warrior Arjuna about his conduct on the field of battle. With this principle we can view not only our ordinary activities of everyday life, but also our religious activity in an entirely new way — not as something done to achieve a result.

WHY DO IT?

Of course, people then ask, "Why do it?"

People are always asking why, but one must realize that *why* is a barren question. You expect an answer addressed in terms of motivation: you want to know the cause of what somebody is doing, and the goal it leads to. If you are acting without a goal in mind, however, you can't say why you're doing it, except to do it.

Yet people are still bothered, and ask, "Why do it then?" — as if to say, "Why use energy at all? Why not just be still?" But of course that's the same as asking, "Why does the universe exist?" Why, in other words, is there motion?

The answer to that is because there is stillness. And why is there stillness? Because there is motion. In this way you reach an end to the question *why,* because it just goes around in circles.

Another way to reach an end to the question *why* is to go back into the past, because when you do you find explanations behind explanations, so that, in the words of a favorite semanticists' verse:

> *Big explanations have little explanations*
> *upon their backs to bite them,*
> *and little explanations have lesser explanations,*
> *and so on infinitum.*

In other words, you can never get there.

What happens, in fact, when we search the past to try to understand why we are doing what we are doing? What happens is that the track fades away. Look back as far as you may, but you will never find the beginning because the track gives out, just as the wake of a ship vanishes, or the contrail of a plane melts into the air.

The past, which we considered to be the push-off point, or the cause, is gone.

The real reason the past doesn't work as an explanation, however, is of course very simple: the push-off, the cause, never was in the past, it has always been in the present. It is perfectly obvious that if there was a time when the universe came into being, when it did do so, it was *now*. And that now is still here, and it is still beginning, right at this moment. So what we call the past is simply the traces, the fade-outs trailing away from the present.

So there is little point in asking why you are here, because unless you think you are here to resolve some past business — in which case you have been motivated as if you were a billiard ball hit by a cue — the issue is irrelevant.

Everybody is always talking about motivation and asking why, "Why do it?" But you can always say, "Why not?" And although that sounds a little childish by way of an answer, there *is* no why, and in a way that is rather splendid.

We tend to think that things are meaningless and dreadful if we can't explain why they happen. A policeman who pulls over a motorist who wasn't going fast enough asks, "Where are you going?" "Nowhere special," comes the answer. This irritates the policeman because he thinks you must be on the road for some reason, and that you ought to be going somewhere. If you are not, you are suspect because you're probably crazy or up to no good.

DESIRES AND DRIVES

Why do you do anything? Is it because of desire?

When people refer to their basic desires, they call them instincts, which is simply a way to label desires as drives. We all feel driven — and yet you don't realize that the energy of a drive is *you*. When you habitually abstract yourself from what you are experiencing as the experiencer or the knower of the experience, you come to feel like a puppet being driven by your emotions, or by your appetites or desires, whatever they are. But in fact they do not drive you, for there is no you to be driven by them. They *are* you.

And so this notion that leads to saying or thinking, "Excuse me, I am driven," or "Excuse me, I have to eat, I have to work, I have sexual desires" — all this is rubbish. I will not apologize for what is called "my hunger." I am very happy to be hungry, and to eat. So instead of saying, "Excuse me, but I must eat," I eat with pleasure. Look at what a degradation of ourselves that attitude carries with it, and it all comes from this feeling of being pushed or driven by something we believe is greater than we are.

THE VAST WORKINGS UNDERNEATH

The reason we feel it is greater than ourselves is because we have a conception of ourselves as nothing more than the superficial scanning mechanism called "consciousness." Of course, if that is all you are, naturally you feel driven, because you are disconnecting yourself from the vast workings that lie behind consciousness.

We disown the part of ourselves that we call instinctual, animal, or primitive. We think instead that as human beings we are the garnishing on top of the evolutionary pile. We feel we are much more evolved, not realizing that everything we have by way of consciousness and reason grows out of the primal energy that lies underneath it.

Therefore, if reason grows out of the primal energy that we are, then it means that the primal energy is at least reasonable, whatever else it may be. You can tell the tree by its fruits — for "by their fruits you shall know them" — and so it is that figs do not grow on thistles, or grapes on thorns, and a stupid universe does not create people. People are a manifestation of the potentiality in the energy of the universe, and if we are intelligent, then that which we express is also intelligent. By logical extension, that in which we express it is our central self. The world is not something external; it is what is most fundamentally you.

As long as we think we are motivated by something

external, however, and therefore feel insufficient, as long as we have that conception of ourselves, we are playing to win, because what we want is to win more, and become more. But as I pointed out, our conception or image of ourselves is only a caricature, and as such is abstract and completely inadequate. It feels as if we're insufficient in some way.

If you ask, "What did you do yesterday?" the average person will consult memory and give you a very attenuated, strung-out chronicle of events, having reduced yesterday's experience to a thin line of words. What you did yesterday becomes what you noticed yesterday, and what you noticed yesterday was a very tiny part of what happened. It was only as much as you could record in some memory code, in words or in brief impressions.

If you identify yourself with that skinny little stream of life, it is no wonder that you feel unsatisfied, because you ate the fish bones instead of the fish. And since we think that is what is happening all the time, and that life is only this skinny little thing, we feel hungry for experience, for thrills, and for ecstasy.

We say, "There must be more coming," and we need more and more future, because the past is gone, and it was a scraggly past anyway. We have no present, because life looks like an hourglass: It has a big future and a big past, but only a tiny little neck of a present that everything is squeezed through.

In Buddhist symbology the idea behind the hour-glass is represented as a kind of being called a *preta*. A preta is thought of as a hungry spirit, and these creatures are represented as having enormous bellies but mouths and throats only about the diameter of a needle, so they can never get enough. That tiny mouth and immense belly represents the neck of the hourglass, and the feeling of having no present.

In fact, our present is enormously rich, and you will realize this if you understand that there is no time except present time. There is only now; there never was any time but now, and there never will be any time but now. It is all now. There is no hurry to gobble life down, and if you do you won't be able to digest it. We can go on much longer than we suppose without eating, so it's all right to just sit and be in the present.

But if you identify with the linear conception of yourself, with your story, and with the abstract ego, you feel inadequate, and therefore it becomes necessary to try to make up for that inadequacy by using energy to attain more in all sorts of ways.

WANTING MORE CONTROL

We want more control over what happens, and this leads us through a progression of steps. We start of course by attempting to acquire power in a physical way, through the possession of material wealth, historically of cattle, of slaves, of land, of crops. Then to retain all that and keep command over people's minds, we construct societies to dole out this material wealth.

But as everybody who has ever had this kind of wealth knows, it doesn't stop the feeling of inner frustration. We notice that when wealth has been in a family for a few generations, the descendants of the original robber baron become spiritual, and they go into the arts and into religion because they still feel unsatisfied. Of course, many people who have never been through the phase of having material wealth have nontheless understood that it is a blind alley, and gone into the arts or religion right away.

THE FIRST PHASE OF RELIGION: SIMPLE MAGIC

Religion in its first phase, however, is what we call "simple magic" and is typified by the attempt to control the world not by the violence of arms and muscular strength, but by hypnotizing it and enchanting it. Women sometimes control men by enchanting them, and men try to control women by a similar process — and throughout history, religion has been an attempt to enchant the universe, to enchant the gods by offering sacrifices and through religious dances and rituals. Thus religion becomes magical religion.

People ask a person who goes to church, particularly if they go to a church where they practice magic, "Why do you do that? Why do you have to do those rituals?" The answer inevitably is, in one way or another, "We perform these rites because we believe they are pleasing to God, and we have been ordered to do these things. This is the way it has been revealed that we should worship, and therefore we do it, hoping of course that God will bless us with long life, health and wealth, and sons and daughters." In this sense, all of this is still being done out of a feeling of inadequacy.

THE MORAL PHASE OF RELIGION

A more sophisticated phase of religion comes into play when the prophet finally says, "Your burnt offerings are an offense to me. Your feast days and your rites are all foolish. What I require is justice and mercy towards other people." Then religion passes from a magical phase into a moral phase, in which the emphasis is placed on living and loving, the building up of human solidarity and community.

At this level the teacher of religion becomes primarily the prophetic teacher of morals, but unfortunately you cannot love out of aridity. If you have an arid identity, you have no love to give. If you conceive yourself to be this cut-off plant that we call the conscious ego, you have no roots into a rich and luscious soil, and so all you have to give is just a little surface energy; you have no deep and abiding love.

As a result, the moral preachings are given to people who are perfectly incapable of observing them. The preachers will tell you how you ought to behave, specifically what you should do and what you should not do, but they never tell you how to become the kind of person who can do those things. And so all they succeed in is making matters worse by making you feel guilty and inadequate. You know you should do what they say, but you can't figure out for the life of you how to do it, and so you feel guilty.

A person who feels guilty feels more deprived than ever, and so has to resort to all sorts of measures to assuage their sense of guilt. Naturally this does not work, and then we begin to see that religion must involve more than moral precepts.

GRACE: THE TRANSFORMING POWER OF THE DIVINE

Religion must be a way of putting us in touch with what the Christians call "grace" — that is to say, the transforming power of the divine. Of course, they usually turn this around and say you will receive grace through magic, and so they practice the magic ceremonies of Baptism and Holy Communion. It is thought that if you participate in these ceremonies in the proper way, the magical power of God will come through and will change you. But it somehow does not seem to do so. In that situation the Buddhists and Hindus might say that the magic failed because it was not performed properly — because you were in the wrong frame of mind.

Jesus essentially said the same thing: If you will have faith, it will work. But somehow you have to find faith, and how do you find faith when you don't have it? If you ask that question of the preachers and the priests, they don't know how to answer. They may write very clever books to persuade you that God really does exist and that it is quite scientific to believe in God, but they cannot instill faith. The more cleverly you reason it out, the more all this implies doubt, and the very need to resort to clever reasoning assures us there is no genuine expression of faith.

THE PRACTICE OF MEDITATION

On this level of religion you find the quest to transform consciousness through the practice of meditation.

One may have heard that by fasting or by concentrating on breathing there is a way of opening oneself up to higher energies. One may believe that as these energies course through you they produce a magical power — and so therefore we learn what is essentially self-hypnosis, and it can do some very startling things.

However, we soon come back to the same problem we found with the geneticists, who can also do some very startling things. As all skilled technologists know, the question is, What are you going to do with it? Do you know what to do when you acquire power through meditation? How are you going to use it?

And the question still is, Who are you? Who is going to decide how to use it? Who is getting this power?

Of course, at the back of your mind you still have the attenuated and impoverished conception of you and the feeling of chronic tension that holds on tight and is the basis for the feeling of "I," of ego. There are teachers of sensory awareness who can show you how to relieve that chronic tension so you can relax and let go of the experience of being an ego for a while. That is very nice, of course, but soon afterward you relapse once again into that tension.

As long as you believe that you are your image of yourself and that you can govern your thoughts and your feelings, you will relapse into the habit of making muscular tensions to control yourself, and you will experience the ego illusion all over again. Then you may feel guilty because you are not relaxing, and the minute you feel guilty you can be certain that the ego is operating very well, although this guilty feeling means it feels injured. The ego's pride has been hurt, and no amount of guilt will get rid of the underlying problem.

At this point you may begin to realize that the meditation exercises are still a form of magic done to aggrandize yourself, and that like preachers and teachers who inculcate a sense of guilt, you are simply trying to quench thirst with salt water.

The problem is that the self-improvement approach is based on an experience of yourself that is completely inadequate. So long as you are the thinker separate from the experience of thoughts, the feeler separate from the experience of feelings, or the experiencer separate from the experience, you will feel strangled like the neck of the hungry spirit, the neck of the hourglass.

In trying to make improvements, that is the way you've defined yourself, and therefore you will not be able to use energy joyously because you will be using it with an ulterior motive. In approaching "the problem," you have defined yourself as a motivated and driven being, as a puppet.

When this illusion dissolves, however, you will discover something very strange — that meditation and religious and spiritual exercises of any kind are not necessary. People always ask if it is necessary to learn yoga breathing, or to practice tai chi, or to be psychoanalyzed. And I always ask, "Necessary for what? Where are you going? What do you want?"

Yes, if you want to get to New York it may be necessary to take the freeway. But where are you going? And what do you mean by *necessary?* Is it necessary for becoming a Buddha? Does anybody want to be a Buddha? Do you know what it means to be a Buddha?

How do you know you want to be a Buddha if you don't know what a Buddha is?

People think it would be nice to have peace of mind, to be serene, to be calm, to be undisturbed by this, that, and the other. But as long as you make all those things objects of desire, you have defined yourself as lacking them, and a person who is looking for peace is obviously in turmoil.

The person who is looking to end conflict is in conflict, and so the more you strive to stop the interior commotion, the more you are stirring it up. You are trying to smooth the waters with an iron, and it will never work.

WHY DO YOU MEDITATE?

Invariably at this point the big question arises: "If you are going to tell us that meditation is not necessary, and that it is all here and now, then why do you meditate? Why do you practice religion, perform rituals, or chant? Why do you even talk about it?"

My answer is that there is no good reason for it whatsoever. This is all a form of joyous energy, and to play with it is a form of dance. It is a great thing to do, and there are all kinds of great things to do, and we are free to explore according to our own tastes.

You can make any human activity into meditation simply by being completely with it and doing it just to do it. If you really enjoy swimming, you swim not to get to the other side of a river, or to complete a certain number of laps, or to go so far out into the ocean, or to compete in any way with yourself or with other people. You swim to experience the water rippling past you, and to enjoy the floating sensation when you lie on your back and look at the blue sky and the birds circling about. Every moment of it you are simply absorbed in this ripply, luminous world, looking at the patterns and the shifting net of sunlight underneath, and the sand way down below — that's what swimming is about.

Some of us like swimming, and in the same way some of us like religion and meditation.

A MAGNIFICENT ART FORM

We have gone through all the levels of religion until we arrive at the religion of nonreligion, where we can see that it was all here anyway and there was nothing that had to be done. In the same spirit we can then go back through the rest of life and turn it into an art form — and it is a magnificent art form.

But if you ask me why you should choose that expression rather than some other, I won't have an answer for you, except to say that getting together and meditating or chanting is what a lot of people did before they had television to absorb them.

In the jungles and on the terraces in mountain communities, for as long as anyone can remember people have gotten together to do a thing I call "digging sound." Some people still play with this sonic energy of the universe, in just the same way as I described somebody playing with the water while swimming. When these people do this, they don't worry about where they are going, or what their destiny is, or any such nonsense. Instead, they are completely alive.

A Vast Celebration

To better understand all that I am trying to say, I would like to ask if you would for the moment change your basic notions of economics — and by this I mean the economics of energy. We are always scrimping and saving because our economic models are based on scarcity rather than exuberance. But notice that the economics of nature are allegedly wasteful by our standards, and they are based on exuberance. Many more seeds than are necessary for trees and many more spermatozoa than are necessary for people are produced, and there are many more stars than anybody could conceivably want, with galaxies galore. Nature is a vast celebration of energy.

If you complain about this and say, "Oh dear me, it's all going to run out," that only means you are still looking for fulfillment in the future. Essentially you are saying, "If there is not enough future, we won't get the golden reward we are looking forward to at the end of the line."

At the heart of our economic model is a view of time that is strung out on a line, but in the natural world everything happens in cycles, which is to say in circles. Life moves through the cycles of birth, growth, flowering, and bearing fruit, which in turn casts the seed that begins life. The flowering is our symbol for the exuberance of life, and the fruits the enjoyment of its abundance.

In religious art, the golden flower represents fulfillment, and when a human being tries to symbolize what it is that they really want at the end of the line, very often they think of a flower. It is there in the celestial rose in Dante's vision of paradise, and in the golden lotus of Mahavairocana, the great Sun Buddha at the center of the mandala. There are rose windows in cathedrals, and always that flower at the end of the line.

Freud says of the flower that it is where everybody wants to go, and, being Freud, he says it is going back to the womb. What is so attractive about the womb? To explain the religious imagery of the flower by analogy with sex is only to add another puzzle. What is so great about sex? What's so great about going back to the womb? There we are regressed to the place that psychologists don't really like to talk about, and they may say that in the womb the baby feels omnipotent, but this is of course a fantasy.

We have assumed the Darwinian struggle for existence as our personality, and say of the exuberance of flowers and the abundance of fruit that they flourish only to ensure survival — but this is truly an impoverished view of life, a secular view in which the person in the world is divorced from the womb. In the womb the baby floats, and the floating baby does not know the difference between what is inside its skin and what is outside. It has what Freud calls the "oceanic feeling," and this is just another form of cosmic consciousness, only the baby does not have the language to express it like an adult. Yet there it is, drifting in the cosmic ocean — and in a way that *is* what everybody wants, because that is our original nature.

Oscar Wilde described the womb-flower of existence as "the flowers in which the gold bees dream." Yet that golden flower isn't at the end of the line — you are living in it. The radiating petals, the mandala, the great circle of the flower is the galaxy in which you live, and it is the whole universe radiating around you. Of course, this radiance is also in a cycle, and that cycling is the dance you are intimately involved in, if you can only realize that the purpose of life is not in the future.

Of course, if you think it is in the future, you will go on and on looking for it there and never find it. The future fades away in the same way the past fades out. You get older and older, and the future never comes, and you just peter out. It was never there, and you may feel vaguely cheated about the whole thing. You thought that there was something coming, that there was some great thing at the end of the line, the golden reward.

And you have been sitting in the middle of that golden reward all the time.

Now all this should be very easy to understand, unless you take a masochistic view and you feel that if you do not suffer the experience is not real. Everybody seems to be looking for new ways of suffering, as if there weren't enough in life anyway, and trying to get in touch with their "authentic" existence. But in fact, whether you're in touch with your authentic existence or not, you can't lose it, so there is no need to worry about losing the feeling of it, no need to say, "I know it's there because I've seen it once, but I am afraid I will lose the feeling of it."

Just forget about it. When you are trying to feel it — as if you couldn't — that is pushing it away. You can't get rid of your real self any more than you can get rid of now. It *is* you. It's your being — to be more accurate, your being is not your being, *you* are the being. It doesn't matter if you live or die; it doesn't make the slightest difference. It is nothing just as much as it is something, and nothing and something are simply the alternations and the vibration of energy.

WHAT DOES IT FEEL LIKE AT THIS MOMENT?

How are you feeling now? Just feel yourself. What does it feel like just to be here now? Just feel the feeling — and can you feel, in addition to this feeling, someone feeling it, or is that the same as the feeling?

Some of you may have what you would call negative feelings — depression, anxiety — and you may feel tension in the chest, a funny feeling in the stomach, or pressure in the head. Or if you are sick in a chronic way, you may feel trouble from the center where the sickness is located. But, at this moment, don't name that feeling — just explore it. It is there, whatever it is. Now you may want to change that feeling, but suppose you can't. For a while you may be able to think about something else, but now let's say to ourselves, "I feel the way I feel, and I can't really do much about it." As we have seen, that is because the "I" that is supposed to be separate from and controlling the feeling is only imaginary.

INNER AND OUTER WORLDS

So if that is the case, then what you are is the totality of this present experience — the inner feelings, the discomfort and rumblings and pulsations inside your organism, together with your outer feelings, because actually your outer sensations are happening inside your brain. What you see out in front of you is the state of your optical nerves, which are inside your head. What you hear is the state of your auditory nerves, which are inside your head. So inner and outer are really so mixed up with each other that there is no difference.

The skin is the bridge between the world "inside the skin" and the world "outside the skin." But there would be no external world if there weren't an internal one, and vice versa. Your internal world is in my external world, and my internal world is in your external world. It all goes together in a great mixed sensory field where everything is essential to everything else, like backs to fronts and fronts to backs.

So here it is, and you can feel everything happening. Your breath is going along. Your ears are working. The people across from you are moving, the trees and buildings are coloring and shaping. It is all that kind of a happening.

Now we can equally well define this happening as your doing. This whole happening that is going on — that is you, if there is a you, a self, in any sense whatsoever. So if you try to change it, you are differentiating yourself from it. You are standing away from it and, in that moment, you split the unity.

But don't worry if you find yourself habitually

standing away from it. Simply treat that as part of the happening. If you can't stop standing away from it — objectifying it, as it were — that is also part of the happening and it is going on. If there are some things you can't accept, and you are fighting them, that fighting is part of the happening too. So don't try to interfere with it, just let be whatever is.

There is no hurry, and no place else to be. I suppose you can go away if you want to, if you are nervous and want to do something else. But has it occurred to you that there may be really nowhere to go, because you take yourself with you if you go somewhere else? And if you have a problem here, you will have a problem somewhere else, because you are the problem. So there is no hurry, and in a way there is no future. It is all here — so take it easy, take your time, and get acquainted with it.

Watch Quietly

Just watch quietly this "going on." Whether you close your eyes or keep them open makes little difference. You find yourself once again tending to put names, words, descriptions on everything that you experience, and that's not necessary. Don't try to stop yourself putting names on things, just regard your doing that as an activity that is happening, like the sound of a car going by. If you ask, "Why am I doing this?" just hear the sound — "why am I doing this, why am I doing this" — as "da da da, dadada."

When you feel those outside sounds and activities and motions, they may seem strange because they are no longer under your voluntary control — but neither are your belly rumbles or the mechanisms of your optical nervous system. None of this is under your control, but it is all definitely you. The idea that you control something really isn't under your control either, because when we move our fingers, we're using energy, but we don't control that energy. Our thoughts are just energy too — it is all bubbling up in us, and we don't know why.

In the same way, all the happenings that are by social definition outside your skin — not under your voluntary control and so not you — are just as much you as the belly rumbles and the energy bubbling up inside you. This whole experience is you going along, and if you try to control it, you will again begin all sorts of absurd straining, like trying to lift an airplane off the ground by pulling at your seat belt. So just let all this that you are feeling happen, because in fact there is nothing else you can do. There is no choice; it is going to happen anyway.

YOUR FULL BODY, YOUR REAL SELF

Now in this state it is your full body that you are experiencing, the whole body of your experience.

In the Far East, the Buddhists say that our full body, our real body, is composed of a trinity of three bodies: *Nirmanakaya* is the functioning body, the physical body with which we usually identify. *Sambhogakaya* is the body of our mental and emotional activity, and it is our capacity to enjoy, for it is the energy of eternal delight. *Dharmakaya* is our ultimate body, our real body, which consists of nothing less than the whole quantum field of the universe, for, in truth, we are One with All That Is.

Feel it, it is happening.

Your wandering thoughts are just happening. The buzz in the head is just happening. There you are.

It is not being pushed around by anything. It is the big happening, and that means it's free. It isn't happening *to* you, it is you happening, and that's the difference.

Meet your real self.

PART II

THE ESSENTIAL PROCESS
OF MEDITATION

CHAPTER THREE

THE PHILOSOPHY OF MEDITATION

I AM BY NATURE a person who has the fundamental feeling that existence is extremely odd.

Other people apparently think that existence is quite even — that is to say, ordinary — and not to be questioned, but I have always had in the bottom of my heart the sense that it is very strange indeed that I am here at all. The feeling of "I" gives me what I can only describe as a funny feeling, and I do not take it for granted.

This feeling is not something that I can just toss off, and then go on with my everyday business — and yet the curious paradox of this is that, at the same time, I do not take it seriously. On one hand I have the feeling that to be alive, to participate in this universe, is so wonderful I simply don't know what

81

to say about it, but on the other I can't identify myself with any of the parts or the social roles that people play.

THE PROBLEM WITH EXISTENCE

There does seem to be a problem with existence, and with being alive. What that problem is about, at the sort of nitty-gritty level, is the very basic idea in our thinking that one must live, that we need to survive to go on, and therefore we need money for food and shelter. We feel we must go on, even though we know that we are not going to get away with it for very long, and we know that after a certain number of years we are going to die and that this thing we call life is going to end.

When life ends the thing that we call "I" is going to go somewhere else, maybe into a deep sleep, maybe even without dreams. Between now and that inevitable event we may experience the most ghastly pains — not only the pains of physical disease, or of being wounded or hurt, but perhaps the pains of worrying about the failure of our responsibility to people who depend on us. So we suffer other people's suffering simply because we are sensitive and have imagination; we do it so much that our adrenaline levels respond simply by imagination to the sufferings of other people.

Obviously all these problems cannot be solved on the physical level — we don't expect in our lifetime that medical skill will make us exempt from death. We also don't seriously expect that human beings will all learn to be nice to each other, and will refrain from war, racial prejudice, and horrors of that kind. We don't seriously expect to find a method of being protected against all possible disease and pain by taking some sort of drug.

ANOTHER WAY AROUND THESE PROBLEMS

Over the years I have begun to wonder if there is another way around these problems. Perhaps instead of resolving these issues at the technical level, we could solve them at the psychological and spiritual levels by disciplining ourselves so that we wouldn't be afraid of them anymore. And so, in accord with that motivation, we seek out spiritual and psychological teachers.

We wonder if we could somehow be made over so that we would not have to worry about our problems. But if you examine the desire to overcome this mess through a spiritual discipline, you will see that this wanting to overcome the mess and not to have it anymore is precisely the mess. The thing that we object to about ourselves is precisely what we continue to do in our attempts to overcome it; in other words, the activity that we employ in overcoming the mess is the mess that we object to. It is very important to realize this, and if you do realize it, it raises the question "Then what can I do?" What can I do to transform this quaking mess into the state of mind of the true mystic?

Now, if you are the mess, there is obviously nothing that you can do to transform yourself into the state of mind you idealize as that of a true mystic, a saint, or even the Christ. But by pursuing this line of thought you may realize that all your ideals are simply manifestations of the mess trying to get away from itself.

You are put in the position of feeling that it is absolutely necessary to be different from the way you are, but there is absolutely nothing you can do about it because being the way you are, you can't be different from your self. It's as if one were to say, "I know that I shouldn't be selfish, and I would very much like to be an unselfish person, but the reason why I want to be an unselfish person is that I am very selfish. And really I would love myself far more and respect myself far more if I were unselfish."

The same is true of people who believe that they ought to love God. One might well ask, "Why do you want to love God?" And the answer is invariably, because God is the most powerful ruler, and it is always best to be on the side of the big battalions. Most often that is the real reason why people believe in God, and it comes down to the fact that they are looking out for the safety of their own spiritual skins.

All sophisticated saints have known this, including Saint Paul, Saint Augustine, and Martin Luther. None of these great men knew what to do about this contradiction, because if people believe in it there is really nothing to be done. But apparently something has to be done — however, when you really look into yourself, you realize there is nothing you can do. There is nothing anyone can do to be anyone else than who they are, or to feel any other way than the way they feel at this moment.

We are this mess that has the capacity to know the horrors of what life can do to us — yet this is not as much of a blind alley as it seems to be. If you discover yourself in a blind alley, or even a cul-de-sac, the fact that you found yourself there will invariably tell you something.

Watch the flow of water when it floods an area of land and you will see that it puts out fingers, and some of them stop because they come to blind alleys. But the water doesn't pursue that course; it simply finds its way around. The water never uses any effort, however, only its weight and gravity, and by following its level it finds the path of least resistance.

As human beings we do the same thing, and when we think that we have come to a dead end or a blind alley we try to find another way around. Suppose the water, when it reaches a place where a finger of water stretches out over dry ground and doesn't go further, were to say to itself, "I failed!" Why, we would say it was just being neurotic. "Just wait," we would advise, "and you will find the way to get through."

Now when you discover that you are like the water, and that there is no way of transforming yourself, you become a fearless, joyous, divine being, as distinct from a quaking mess.

When you see that there is no way, it is not a gloomy realization, but a very important communication. It is telling you something in the same way that the land is telling the water this is not the way to go. It is really saying, "There is another way — try over here."

Sometimes life is telling you that the course you are on is not the way to go, and the message underlying all of this is that you cannot transform yourself. Life is giving you the message that the "you" that you imagine to be capable of transforming yourself does not exist. In other words, as an ego, I am separate from my emotions, my thoughts, my feelings, my experiences. So the one who is supposed to be in control of them cannot control them because it isn't there. And as soon as you understand that, things will be vastly improved.

What Do You Mean by the Word "I"?

Now we can go into this and ask, "What do you mean by the word 'I'?" We are going to try some experiments on a number of different levels, first in the ordinary way: What do you mean by the word "I"? I, myself. Your personality, your ego — what is it?

First of all, it is your image of yourself, and it is composed of what people have told you about yourself. Who you are is based upon how others have reacted to you, and what sort of impression they have given you of the kind of person you are. Your education plays into the process as well, and out of all this an ego emerges that is a conceptual expression of who you think you are. The style of life you then live is a reflection of this image.

But remember, it is an image — just an idea. It is your thoughts about yourself, but in fact you are not this at all. Your total physical organism, your psychological organism, and forces beyond that are all you, because an organism doesn't exist as an isolated entity any more than a flower exists without a stalk, without roots, without earth, without the environment.

In the same way, although we are not stalked to the ground, we are nevertheless inseparable from the world around us, and from a huge social context of parents, siblings, and people who know us and work with us. It is simply impossible to cut ourselves off from either our social environment or our natural environment. We are all that, and there is no clear way of drawing the boundary between this organism and everything that surrounds it.

And yet, the image of ourselves that we have does not include all those relationships. Our idea of our personality and of ourselves includes no information whatsoever about the hypothalamus or even the brain stem, the pineal gland, the way we breathe, how our blood circulates, how we manage to form a sentence, how we manage to be conscious, or even how we open and close our hands. The information contained in your image of yourself says nothing about any of this.

Therefore it is obviously an extremely inadequate image, but nonetheless we do think that the image of self refers to something because we have the very strong impression that "I" exist. And we think that this impression isn't just an idea, it is really substantially there, right in the middle of us. And what is it?

What do you actually sense? When you are sitting on the floor, you feel the floor is there and is real and hard. What is the "you" sitting on the floor, and what do you have the sensation of when you know that it's you, right here? What is it?

First of all, let's ask, "In what part of your body do you feel your self — the real "I" — exists?" We can explore this question very deeply, and maybe you want to think about it for a moment before I suggest a preliminary and superficial answer:

The sensation that corresponds to the feeling of "I" is a chronic muscular tension in the body, which has absolutely no function whatsoever.

What do you do when you try, or concentrate, or pay attention? When I was a little boy in school I sat next to another boy who had great difficulty in reading. And as he worked over the textbook with its perfectly piffling information, he groaned and grunted as he read, trying to get the sounds out, as if he were heaving enormous weights with his muscles. The teacher was vaguely impressed that he was trying, and although he seemed to be making a tremendous effort, all of his straining had absolutely nothing to do with getting anything done.

Tying yourself up into a knot has absolutely nothing to do with the way your mind works. If you try very hard, and look very intensely, perhaps you will tighten the muscles around your temples, and maybe clench your jaw a bit, but if it does anything, it will just make your vision blurry. If you want to see something clearly, you relax, and instead of making an effort you simply trust your eyes and your nervous system to do their job.

The other night I was writing and I completely forgot somebody's name, but I knew that eventually my memory would produce it. I just sat for a while and said to my memory, "You know very well who this person is, please give me the answer." And there it was, because that's the way nerves work. They don't work by forcing themselves, and yet we've all been brought up to try to force our nervous activity, our concentration, our memory, our comprehension, and indeed our very love.

We have tried to force it with our muscles — and

men will understand me if I say you can't force yourself to have an erection by muscular effort. Women will understand me if I say you can't force yourself with muscles to have an orgasm — it just has to happen, and you must trust it to happen. There is absolutely nothing you can do about it by using your muscles. In much the same way, the notion that we have of ourselves, of ego, is a composite of an image of ourselves that doesn't fit the facts, and a sensation of muscular straining that is futile. When you come down to it and take a closer look, what you conceive to be yourself is the marriage of an illusion and futility.

WE ARE NO LESS THAN THE UNIVERSE

Well what are we, if we aren't who we think we are? When you take a scientific point of view, your organism is inseparable from its environment, and so you really are the organism/environment. In other words, you are no less than the universe, and each one of you is the universe expressed in the particular place that you feel is here and now. You are an aperture through which the universe is looking at itself and exploring itself.

When you feel that you are a lonely, put-upon, isolated little stranger confronting all this, you are under the influence of an illusory feeling, because the truth is quite the reverse. You are the whole works, all that there is, and always was, and always has been, and always will be. But just as my whole body has a little nerve end centered here, which is exploring and which contributes to the sense of touch, you are just such a little nerve end for everything that is going on. Just as the eyes serve the whole body, you serve the entire universe. You are a function of all that is.

Yet if this is so, the facts just do not fit the way we feel, because we feel it the other way around: "I am a lonely little thing out here exploring this universe and trying to make something out of it. I want to get something out of it and do something with it. And I know I am going to fail because I know I'm going to die one day." So we are all fundamentally depressed, and as a result think up fantasies about what is going to happen to us when we are dead, and try to make ourselves feel better about it.

But if you are essentially the universe, what is going to happen to you when you are dead?

What do you mean by *you?* If you are the universe, in the greater context that question is irrelevant. You never were born and you never will die, because what there is, is you. That should be absolutely obvious, but from an egoistic perspective it is not obvious at all. It should be the simplest thing in the world to understand that you, the "I", is what has always been going on and always will go on, coming and going forever and ever.

We have been bamboozled, however, by religionists,

by politicians, by our fathers and mothers, by all sorts of people who tell us, "You're not it." And we believed it.

So, to put it in a negative way, you can't do anything to change yourselves, to become better, to become happier, to become more serene, to become more mystical. But if I say you can't do a damn thing, you can understand this negative statement in a positive way. What I am really saying is that you don't need to do anything, because if you see yourself in the correct way, you are all as much extraordinary phenomena of nature as trees, clouds, the patterns in running water, the flickering of fire, the arrangement of the stars, and the form of a galaxy. You are all just like that, and there is nothing wrong with you at all.

An Element of Doubt

You may have an element of doubt in you, however. We all object to ourselves in various ways, and in a sense there is nothing wrong with that either, because that is part of the flow, of what is going on. That is part of nature, and a part of what we do. To deliver you from the sense of guilt, I am going to teach you that you needn't feel guilty because you feel guilty.

They taught you as a child to feel guilty, and you feel guilty — that's no surprise. If somebody comes along and says you shouldn't, that is not the point. I am not going to say that you shouldn't — but I say that if you do, don't worry about it. And if you want to say, "But I can't help worrying about it," I'm going to say, "Okay, go ahead and worry about it."

This is the principle called judo in Japanese, which means the gentle way. Go along with it, go along with it — and then you can redirect the energy to go your own way.

The most interesting thing you can do in life is really the most natural thing to do: to call into question the rules of the game. If we say, "Let's all be honest with each other," what do you mean by honesty? Do you know what the truth is?

If you call these things into question, a curious thing happens, and that is that nobody knows what they are supposed to do. And this is the most embarrassing situation in life. When we are all here and we don't know what we're supposed to do, now we are really up against our view of reality.

THE ESSENTIAL PROCESS OF MEDITATION

This is the beginning of meditation. You don't know what you're supposed to do, so what can you do? Well, if you don't know what you're supposed to do, you watch. You simply watch what is going on.

When somebody plays music, you listen. You just follow those sounds, and eventually you understand the music. The point can't be explained in words because music is not words, but after listening for a while, you understand the point of it, and that point is the music itself.

In exactly the same way, you can listen to all experiences, because all experiences of any kind are vibrations coming at you. As a matter of fact, you are these vibrations, and if you really feel what is happening, the awareness you have of you and of everything else is all the same. It's a sound, a vibration, all kinds of vibrations on different bands of the spectrum. Sight vibrations, emotion vibrations, touch vibrations, sound vibrations — all these things come together and are woven, all the senses are woven, and you are a pattern in the weaving, and that pattern is the picture of what you now feel. This is always going on, whether you pay attention to it or not.

Now instead of asking what you should do about it, you experience it, because who knows what to do about it? To know what to do about this you would have to know everything, and if you don't, then the only way to begin is to watch.

Watch what's going on. Watch not only what's going on outside, but what's going on inside. Treat your own thoughts, your own reactions, your own emotions about what's going on outside as if those inside reactions were also outside things. But you are just watching. Just follow along, and simply observe how they go.

Now, you may say that this is difficult, and that you are bored by watching what is going on. But if you sit quite still, you are simply observing what is happening: all the sounds outside, all the different shapes and lights in front of your eyes, all the feelings on your skin, inside your skin, belly rumbles, thoughts going on inside your head — chatter, chatter, chatter. "I ought to be writing a letter to so-and-so.... I should have done this" — all this bilge is going on, but you just watch it.

You say to yourself, "But this is boring." Now watch that too. What kind of a funny feeling is it that makes you say it's boring? Where is it? Where do you feel it? "I should be doing something else instead." What's that feeling? What part of your body is it in? Is it in your head, is it in your belly, is it in the soles of your feet? Where is it? The feeling of boredom can be very interesting if you look into it.

Simply watch everything going on without attempting to change it in any way, without judging it, without calling it good or bad. Just watch it. That is the essential process of meditation.

CHAPTER FOUR

THE PRACTICE OF MEDITATION

WHAT WE CALL MEDITATION or contemplation — for want of a better word — is really supposed to be fun. I have some difficulty in conveying this idea because most people take anything to do with religion seriously — and you must understand that I am not a serious person. I may be sincere, but never serious, because I don't think the universe is serious.

And the trouble comes into the world largely because various beings take themselves seriously, instead of playfully. After all, you must become serious if you think that something is desperately important, but you will only think that something is desperately important if you are afraid of losing it. In one way, however, if you fear losing something, it isn't really worth having. There are people who live in dread, and then drag on living because they are afraid to die. They will probably teach their children to do the same, and their children will in turn teach their own children to live that way. And so it goes on and on.

But let me ask you, if you were God, would you be serious? Would you want people to treat you as if you were serious? Would you want to be prayed to? Think of all the awful things that people say in their prayers. Would you want to listen to that all the time? Would you encourage it? No, not if you were God.

In the same way, meditation is different from the sort of things that people are supposed to take seriously. It doesn't have any purpose, and when you talk about practicing meditation, it's not like practicing tennis or playing the piano, which one does in order to attain a certain perfection. You practice music to become better at it, maybe even with the idea that you may someday go on stage and perform. But you don't practice meditation that way, because if you do, you are not meditating.

THE PRACTICE OF MEDITATION

The only way you can talk about practice in the context of meditation is to use the word *practice* in the same way as when somebody says that they practice medicine. That is their way of life, their vocation, and they do it nearly every day. Perhaps they do it the same way, day after day — and that's fine for meditation too, because in meditation there is no right way and there is no idea of time.

In practicing and learning things, time is usually of the essence. We try to do it as fast as possible, and even find a faster way of learning how to do things. In meditation a faster way of learning is of no importance whatsoever, because one's focus is always on the present. And although growth may occur in the process, it is growth in the same way that a plant grows.

THE PERFECT PROCESS OF GROWTH

Once upon a time in China, there was a farming family, and they were having dinner. The oldest son came in late, and they asked him, "Why are you late for dinner?"

"Oh," he said, "I've been helping the wheat to grow."

They came out the next morning and all the wheat was dead. It turned out that the son had pulled each stalk up a little bit, to help it grow.

The point is that growth always occurs in a being as it does in a plant, and it is perfect at every step. No progress is involved in the transformation of an acorn into an oak, because the acorn is a perfect acorn, and the sapling is a perfect sapling, and the big oak tree is a perfect oak, which again produces perfect acorns. At every stage perfection is there, and it cannot be otherwise.

Practicing meditation is exactly the same. We should not talk about beginners as distinct from experts, and we should develop, if we can, a new vocabulary because it is very difficult in the context of our competitive world to speak about things like this. To bring across the idea of doing something that is not acquisitive — something you are not going to get anything out of — is difficult. And it's even more difficult when there is no one to get anything. When "you" understand the art of contemplation, there is no experiencer separate from experience, and there is no one to get anything out of life, or therefore to get anything from meditation.

REVERSED EFFORT

We have a principle here of reversed effort, something to understand as a background to anything said about techniques — because whenever we talk about techniques, we seem to be talking about the competitive, and about mastery. The idea of mastery of technique is very important if you play a musical instrument, because technique is the key in the making of a satisfactory sound. But if you force the learning of technique, or force the performance of it, everyone will hear it, and you will hear the forcing yourself.

To be musical you have to address yourself to the

playing of an instrument without hurrying, and without forcing anything. You will find there is a point then where the instrument seems to play itself, and when you get the peculiar feeling that the sound coming out of a flute or a violin string is happening of itself. Then you are playing the instrument properly.

It's the same when you sing: there comes a point when your voice takes over. This is the difference between perspiration and inspiration.

You may say, as Christians do, that the act of worship is inspired by the Holy Spirit. When monks are chanting, they believe that the Holy Spirit is chanting through them, and they are flutes for the Holy Spirit. This is a very precise and particular phenomenon because there is a way of resonating the breath and of harmonizing sound so that it comes of itself and you don't do it. We attribute that way of producing sound to the "Holy Spirit," but it is based on breath.

WATCHING BREATH

Breath is a curious operation, because it can be experienced as both a voluntary doing and an involuntary happening. You can do a breathing exercise and feel that "I am breathing" in just the same way as you can feel "I am walking." Yet on the other hand, you breathe all the time when you are not thinking about it, and in that way it is involuntary. You must breathe —

and so it is the faculty through which we can realize the unity of the voluntary and involuntary systems.

In Buddhism, this is called mindfulness of the breath, or watching breath. And watching breath is fundamental in meditation because, like sound, it is easy to see the happening in it, as distinct from what we thought of as the doing of it. Breath happens, but the curious thing is that you can get with the breath, and in getting with it, extraordinary things can happen.

Anyone who swims knows this, and anyone who sings knows that breathing is important. In archery, in any athletic discipline, the alignment of body and breath is critical. The synchronization of what you are doing with your breathing is the whole art. But powerful breath is not accomplished through muscle power. It is accomplished by gravity, by weight.

A MEDITATION EXERCISE

I would like you to sit upright, either in a comfortable chair or on the floor on a cushion or pillow. The reason for sitting straight is so the part of your body in which the breathing is occurring is unencumbered. Also, when you sit upright on the floor you are slightly uncomfortable, and you won't go to sleep, because in any peaceful and quiet state of mind it is very easy to go to sleep.

Now in this position, simply become aware of your

breathing, without trying to do anything about it at all. Let it happen, and watch it.

At the same time, let your ears hear whatever they want to hear. In other words, let them hear in the same way you are letting your lungs breathe.

Now beyond this, you can breathe out by letting the breath fall outward without pushing it, and as you get to the end of the out breath, let go with the same sort of feeling that you have when you let your body drop into a very comfortable bed — let it drop out and fall. Let the weight of the air do it. Don't push, drop. Then after a while, the breath will return. But don't pull it in, let it fall back in. The breath will drop in until you've had enough; then let it drop out again.

It's a good idea in this exercise to breathe in through the nostrils and out through the lips, allowing there to be a slight sensation of moving air on your lips so that you know you are breathing. Never force anything — just have the feeling of going this way and that way by virtue of weight, and of gravity.

ADDING SOUND

Then, if you wish, as you let the breath fall outward, you can simply float a sound on it. First, you can just do this mentally. Think of a sound that pleases you, a note that seems agreeable to your voice. As you breathe out heavily, imagine that sound to yourself, whatever sound you feel like. Now if you've got a humming sound in mind, on the next round of the out breath, hum it out loud, and keep it going.

At first you may be a little short-winded and uneasy about something like this. As well as allowing the sound to hum and happen with the breath that is falling out, you can, as it were, simply request it to increase in volume without forcing it.

And when your sound ends, bring it in again quite softly, and then allow the volume to rise. You will get an almost continuous sound, and if you do this in a group, the sounds will run together.

Try it now, if you wish, picking your own note.

Try it again, once more.

Now ask it to increase its volume. Listen a moment. What we are working into is the completely liberated, yet soft and gentle, act of letting sound happen through us without the slightest sense of strain, so that you are not singing it, but it is singing with your voice.

Don't premeditate a tune, but let it come, so that it's almost as if you were talking nonsense. Let it play gently with your voice. You are simply preoccupied with it, like easy humming to yourself.

> *Hmmmm....*
> Or, *Ahhh....*
> Or, *Oooommmm....*

When you are thus absorbed in sound, where are you?

You are in a state of consciousness that is, even at first, at least a primitive form of *samadhi;* that is to say, we are happily absorbed in what we are doing, and we have forgotten about ourselves. You can't very well do that and still worry or think about anything serious.

Notice that there is a special way of doing it. We can get wild with it and do a kind of Native American chant or one of the more vigorous and forceful Tibetan Buddhist chants, but that form of chanting can be straining, unless you're in a large group and can soar on the group's energy. If you keep it down to a soft tone, you will find the floating feeling of the voice. If you feel any sound that is uncomfortable, you can instantly avoid it. Slip down if you are going too high, or slip up if you are getting too low. If your voice tends to change, follow its change, so that you are just going along with it.

THE DIVINE ELEMENT

This is why, from ancient times, people have discovered humming and singing, and everybody used to sing while they worked. But you'll notice that today very few people sing at all; you have to make a point of it. People are afraid of their voices — that is, their melodic voices as distinct from the spoken voice. I know an enormous number of people who never sing at all.

In India to this day when the scriptures — the Upanishads and the Sutras — are read, they are invariably chanted, because as soon as you bring a note into it an extra dimension is added to the voice. That is the divine element, which is symbolically the singing sound of the universe.

This is a form of what I would call free mantra chanting, which isn't used much. But as you do it, it will give you a very good idea of what the meditative state is. It isn't just letting things going on around you happen, it is inside you as well. In free mantra, as distinct from prescribed mantra, each spontaneous chant has a different feeling to it.

The Tibetan monks go down to an extraordinarily deep sound — they go as deep as one can get. There is a reason for this, but it is very difficult to explain because you have to do it to understand it. But when you get as deep down into sound as you can go, you are going to an extreme of the vibration, and you feel naturally that what is deep is part of the underpinnings, the foundation. When monks go into that deep sound, they are literally exploring the depths of sound, going into it deeply. They will get down somewhere on an *Om,* and take it to what feels like the center of the earth.

When you try the meditation we have just been through with sound, you might sometimes find that you hear your voice go wrong, but you always get a sensuous feeling of the breath, and of course it is very enjoyable to breathe. You will find this enjoyment will help in the quality of the sound you produce — although we have to get away from some of our musical prejudices when we do this. You can make up your own nonsensical mantras, and there are lots of traditional mantras as well. But to make one up, just absorb yourself in a vibration that gets you going and then play with it.

Play with the sound you are making, and when you stop you will still feel the pulse going through you. These sounds are easy to run along with.

DEEP LISTENING

Some people think that to spend a lot of time gently humming nonsense to yourself is a waste of time. But ask yourself, What are you going to do with the time that you save?

With all this, the first thing we have to understand is what I call deep listening. Very few people ever really listen, because instead of receiving the sound, they make comments on it all the time. They are thinking about it, and so the sound is never fully heard. You just have to let it take over, let it take you over completely, and then you get into the *samadhi* state of becoming it.

This also means that you abandon your socially nervous personality. One of the reasons why people don't sing is that they hear so many masters performing on records that they are ashamed of their own voices. You may think there's no point in singing unless you are good at it, but that is like saying there is no point in doing anything at all unless you are particularly gifted at it, which is ridiculous. Of course singing is very good for you, but we won't dwell on that because it brings too much purposiveness into it — having to fulfill a conscious purpose and design.

ANY SOUND FROM THE SOURCE

Instead we are like children making noises because of the absorbing sound they produce. Children make all sorts of noises to explore the possibilities of what they can do with their voice. But you don't see adults going around humming and burbling, even though it is tremendous fun. All of this is perfectly at home within meditation.

Joshu Sasaki, a Zen master from Los Angeles, tells his students to stand up and laugh for five minutes every morning because that's a better form of meditation than sitting for a long time getting sore legs. It embarrasses the hell out of some people to even try it, and instead when they see someone doing it they ask, "What are you laughing at? You know I don't see any point in laughing unless there's something funny."

I had a friend, a very fat friend, and he was a theological student. He used to take the elevated train that went from Evanston into Chicago and sit in the middle of the car where everybody could see him. He would sit there with a kind of vacant look and chuckle to himself. And slowly he'd work it out, laughing louder and louder with all his flesh vibrating. By the time they got to Chicago, the whole car was inevitably hysterical with laughter.

I tell you this story to illustrate that any sound you feel coming from the inside can be used as mantra meditation, and the deeper the source, now matter how ridiculous, the better.

PART III

STILL THE MIND

CHAPTER FIVE

CONTEMPLATIVE
RITUAL

FOR A LONG TIME, the kind of religious celebrations that we have conducted in the West have been filled with the spoken word and impossibly didactic. Almost all our religious observances are nothing but talk and consist of telling God what to do, as if He or She did not already know, and telling the people what to do, as if they were able or even willing to change. All of this is throwing the book at people, and telling them the Word, and I think we have had enough of it.

The history of religion in the West is nearly equivalent to the history of the failure of preaching. By and large, preaching is a kind of moral violence that excites people's sense of guilt, and there is no less creative sense than that. You cannot love and feel guilty at the same time, any more than you can be afraid and angry at the same time.

A Spiritual Experience

What seems to me to be lacking in our Western religious observances is some sort of ritual that gives us an opportunity for spiritual experience. By a spiritual experience I am referring to a transformation of the individual consciousness so that, in one way or another, the individual is able to realize his oneness with the eternal energy behind this universe, which some people call God and others prefer not to name or to conceive.

When Western people hear that an Asian practices meditation, they ask, "What do you meditate on?" But that question puzzles a Buddhist or a Hindu, because you do not meditate on anything, any more than you breathe on anything. You breathe, and in the same way, you meditate. The verb is in a way intransitive. Meditation is the act of allowing one's thoughts to cease.

Coming Into Touch with Reality

In the beginning of the *Yoga Sutra,* Patanjali described yoga — which means union — as spontaneously stopping the agitation of thinking. Thinking is talking to yourself, or figuring to yourself, and it is habitual for most of us. If I talk all the time, however, I do not hear what anyone else has to say. Equally, if I talk to myself all the time, I will not have anything to think about except thoughts.

There is no interval between thoughts during which I can come into touch with reality — that is to say, the world my thoughts represent, in the way words represent events, or money represents wealth. If I am never silent in my head, I will find myself living in a world of total abstraction divorced from reality altogether.

You may ask, "What is reality?" People have various theories about what it is, but it is important to remember that they are all theories. Those who believe that reality is material are projecting upon the world a certain philosophical theory about it, and those who say that it is mental, or spiritual, are doing likewise.

Reality itself is neither mental nor spiritual, nor any other concept that we can have of it; reality is simply the present moment.

You Cannot Meditate

Words are reality insofar as they are noises, but even that is saying too much. To meditate, you might think that you should attempt to suppress thought, but you don't do that because *you cannot meditate*. Let me repeat that emphatically: you cannot meditate. You, your ego image, can only chatter, because when it stops, it isn't there.

When you are not thinking, you have no ego,

115

because your ego is nothing more than a habitual concept. The thinker behind the thoughts and the feeler behind the feelings are only thoughts; each of these is an idea of some reference point to which all our experiences happen. That thought, however, cuts us off from what we experience and creates the illusion of a gap or gulf between the knower and the known.

This in turn is responsible for the feeling of alienation we have from the world, and as a result we suffer from conflict and hatred. The spirit of domination arises from that basic division that has been constructed in thought, and modern societies are typically obsessed with this highly destructive illusion.

When you come to an end of thought, you don't know how to meditate, and you don't know what to do with your mind, and nobody can tell you. But still, thinking comes to an end naturally, and you just watch.

You don't have to ask who watches because that question merely arises from the fact that in grammar every verb has to have a subject by rule — but that is not a rule of nature, it is a rule of grammar. In nature there can be watching without a separate watcher.

And So You Begin to Meditate

When you realize that you have come to your wit's end, you can begin meditation. Or meditation happens, and that happening is simply the watching of what is, of all the information conveyed to you by your exterior and interior senses, and even the thoughts that keep chattering on about it all.

You don't try to stop those thoughts, you just let them run as if they were birds twittering outside, and they will eventually become tired and stop.

But don't worry about whether they do or don't. Just simply watch whatever it is that you are feeling, thinking, or experiencing — that's it. Just watch it, and don't go out of your way to put any names on it. This is really what meditation is.

You are in meditation in an eternal present, and you are not expecting any result. You are not doing it to improve yourself, because you found that you can't. Your ego can't possibly improve you because it is what's in need of improvement, and your ego can't let go of itself because it is a complex of thoughts called "clinging to one's self." When it is finally understood that it is unable to achieve a transformation of consciousness, or the vivid sense of union of individual and cosmos, it just evaporates.

ONE OF THE EASIEST WAYS TO ENTER IN

One of the easiest ways to enter into the state of meditation, therefore, is listening to what is, and experiencing the qualities of sound.

Curiously enough, sound is a sense that bores us less

easily than sight. When you hear it, just listen to the random sounds that you know are going on in the room, or in the street. Listen as if you were listening to music, without trying to identify its source, to name it, or to put any label on it at all. Just enjoy whatever sound may be going on, whether it is outside or in the area where you are sitting. That is part of the ritual: just listen.

LETTING SOUND HAPPEN THROUGH US

We can go on from that listening to making sound ourselves while also listening to it. But instead of making sound, we will get the knack of letting it happen through us.

Once, a great choirmaster in England was rehearsing a choir in the presence of the archbishop of Canterbury, who was then William Temple, a great theologian. And this was a rather raw choir that didn't really know much about singing. The master gave them a hymn to sing that they knew very well, and to impress the archbishop they sang it with gusto, and it sounded forced and terrible.

Then the choirmaster asked them to sing a little-known hymn and had them go over it several times until everybody got the hang of it. "Now," he said, "I want you to sing this hymn again, but there's one very important thing: don't try to sing it. You mustn't try. You must think of the melody and let it sing itself." And they sang it very well.

Afterward he turned to the archbishop and said, "Your Grace, that's good theology, isn't it?" And it obviously was, since the archbishop told me the story.

MANTRA

In India we find the use of mantra — a mantra is what we would call a chant, where words and sounds are chanted not for their meaning but for their sound. Most mantras are not intended to be understood in a discursive and intellectual sense. Instead, you are asked only to go down into the sound, and the sound penetrates you. You are able to settle right to the bottom of it, because when you are listening to sound, and when you are letting sound hum through you, it is one of the most obvious manifestations of the energy of the universe.

It is commonly said in India that sound is Brahman, sound is God, and perhaps that is the original meaning of saying, "In the beginning was the Word." It did not mean that in the beginning was the chatter, or in the beginning was the commandment or the orders. It meant the vibration, the sound of the word.

So concentrate purely on the sound, and you will find some mantras that play in your ears are so simple that you will be able to join in with them effortlessly, and please do so quite freely.

It is a pity that the Roman Catholic Church, which

used to have a mantric service, is dropping it and putting the Mass in the vernacular, and not particularly good vernacular at that, as far as the English translation is concerned. It has begun to sound terribly intellectual, and often there is somebody standing by the altar with a microphone to explain what's going on, so that it is no longer possible to practice contemplative prayer at Mass. Instead you are hammered with information, with exultation, with edification all the time, and the Catholic Church should realize that in giving up Latin it has lost its magic.

Although we associate mantras with religion, they are not supposed to be understood, because religion is that which is past understanding. Understanding may lead up to it, but to express religion intellectually is to try to use the intellect for something it cannot do. It is comparable to picking up the telephone and dialing W-H-A-T I-S G-O-D, and expecting to get a useful answer. Although the telephone is very useful otherwise, you cannot find out the mystery of the universe through talk — only through awareness.

For that reason I have suggested that churches get rid of their pews, where everybody looks at the backs of each other's necks, and that they spread their floors with rugs and cushions, so that instead of a sermon they have a ritual in which people can approach an ineffable spiritual experience rather than being forced into a particular pattern of thinking.

In this spirit I have only given the slightest suggestion of how one uses the mantra, or the silence, for meditation. You all have your own way of doing things like that, so do it your own way. This technique is a vehicle, or a support for contemplation, and I suggest you simply sit quietly, and when you feel settled proceed into contemplation.

STILL THE MIND

Sit quietly and be with your breath, your mind, and all your feelings.

It doesn't matter whether you are sitting cross-legged or on your knees with your legs folded underneath you. The point is to settle into a posture that is stable and comfortable. You can cross your legs in front of you, or if you are limber you may wish to try the half-lotus or full-lotus position. You can sit on a cushion with your knees bent and legs on either side, or you can sit in a chair. The idea is to be comfortable and find a position that you can maintain effortlessly.

As you settle in, remember that although stillness is emphasized in meditation, this does not mean that you should hold still in a rigid way. Becoming still physically helps one to find stillness of mind, but if you need to move, get comfortable, so that you can settle even more deeply.

Keep your back upright and your head erect, but let

your arms relax. Rest the left palm in the right palm, and put your thumbs together as if you were holding an egg. Your hands should be positioned at your belly with your thumbs just below the navel.

If you are sitting cross-legged you may wish to rock back and forth for a moment to find your natural center. If you are sitting in a chair, plant your feet on the ground so that you are grounded.

Your mouth should be closed, the eyes lowered slightly.

When you have found a stable posture, allow your awareness to sink into your breath and to find the bottom of your breath. You are not trying to cultivate a particular kind of breath; just gently pay attention to your breathing. Allow the breath to come and go as it may.

That's all you need to do. Your body will become still, and your mind will naturally, at some point, become still as well.

That is the essential process of meditation.

If you wish, you can begin to hum when you feel comfortable with it. As your voice rises, begin to play with the sound.

The play of sound will eventually settle into a pattern, and a mantra will spontaneously form. Go with it, and in this moment you are experiencing ritual in its richest form.

ABOUT THE
AUTHOR

ALAN WATTS WAS BORN in England in 1915.
Beginning at age sixteen, when he wrote essays
for the journal of the Buddhist Lodge in London, he
developed a reputation over the next forty years as a
foremost interpreter of Eastern philosophies for the
West, eventually developing an audience of millions
who were enriched through his books, tape recordings, radio and television appearances, and public
lectures. He became widely recognized for his Zen
writings and for *The Book on the Taboo Against
Knowing Who You Are*. In all, Watts wrote more than
twenty-five books and recorded hundreds of lectures
and seminars, all building toward a personal philosophy he shared honestly and joyfully with readers and

listeners throughout the world. His overall works have presented a model of individuality and self-expression that can be matched by few philosophers.

Watts came to the United States in 1938 and earned a master's degree in theology from Seabury-Western Theological Seminary. He was Episcopal Chaplain at Northwestern University during World War II, and held fellowships from Harvard University and the Bollingen Foundation. He became professor and dean of the American Academy of Asian Studies in San Francisco and lectured and traveled widely.

He died in 1973 at his home in northern California, survived by his second wife and seven children.

For more information, and for access to a greater collection of his recorded material, call the Electronic University at (800) 969-2887, or see these websites:

www.alanwatts.com
www.audiowisdom.com

RECOMMENDED
READING

If you enjoyed *Still the Mind,* we highly recommend the following books and cassettes from New World Library:

As You Think by James Allen is a quiet, powerful masterpiece that shows us the greatness we are capable of and gives us the tools to achieve it.

Body Mind Mastery: Creating Success in Sport and Life by Dan Millman offers a regimen that integrates physical training with psychological growth, transforming training into a path of personal growth and spiritual discovery.

Creative Visualization by Shakti Gawain. This pioneering best-seller and perennial favorite teaches methods of meditation and visualization that have proven to have powerful effects on readers' lives.

Living in the Light: A Guide to Personal and Planetary Transformation by Shakti Gawain emphasizes the importance of listening to our intuition and relying on it as a guiding force in our lives.

Meditation for Busy People by Dawn Groves is a concise, jargon-free guide to simple forms of meditation that anyone can practice.

Meditation: The Complete Guide by Patricia Monaghan and Eleanor G. Viereck gives us a clear explanation of more than fifty meditation practices, including the historical background, contemporary use, a description of the practice, and resource lists.

The Seven Spiritual Laws of Success by Deepak Chopra distills the essence of his teachings into simple yet powerful principles that can be easily applied in all areas of your life.

Simple Truths by Kent Nerburn gives us, in simple, moving prose, clear and gentle guidance on the big issues in life.

Stress Reduction and Creative Meditations by Marc Allen is a powerful and popular forty-five-minute audiocassette program. Side One guides us through a deep, complete physical relaxation; Side Two is filled with creative meditations for health, abundance, fulfilling relationships, and attainment of life's purpose.

A Visionary Life: Conversations on Personal and Planetary Evolution by Marc Allen gives readers simple keys to first envision and then move toward realizing their deepest dreams and highest aspirations.

The Wonders of Solitude, edited by Dale Salwak, is a deeply touching volume of more than 300 inspiring and diverse quotations on the nature, importance, and power of solitude.

You Can Be Happy No Matter What by Richard Carlson is the book many consider the finest work to date by the best-selling author of *Don't Sweat the Small Stuff*. The secret to happiness is deceptively simple, for happiness, inner peace, and contentment is our natural state, beyond the mental barriers we have created.